BOOK ANALYSIS

By Steve MacGregor

The Imp of the Perverse

BY EDGAR ALLAN POE

EDGAR ALLAN POE

AMERICAN WRITER AND POET

- **Born in Boston, United States in 1809.**
- **Died in Baltimore, United States in 1849.**
- **Notable works:**
  - *The Narrative of Arthur Gordon Pym of Nantucket* (1838), Poe's only completed novel
  - *The Murders in the Rue Morgue* (1841), short story
  - *The Pit and the Pendulum* (1842), short story
  - *The Raven* (1845), narrative poem

Edgar Allan Poe was an American short story writer, poet, critic, novelist and editor. He is best known for his morbid tales of horror, many of which are now regarded as literary classics. Poe had a turbulent family background, moving often and losing both parents at a young age. He later married his landlady's daughter, Virginia, when she was just 13, and her death nine years later profoundly affected his writing and his emotional state. Poe struggled financially throughout his life until his early death, possibly from TB exacerbated by the effects of alcohol. He popularised American Gothic horror with short stories such as *The Pit and the Pendulum* and is considered the forefather of the modern detective genre with *Murders in the Rue Morgue.* His style has influenced writers such as Baudelaire (French poet, 1821-1867) and Dostoevsky (Russian writer, 1821-1881).

THE IMP OF THE PERVERSE

APOLOGIA FROM A CONDEMNED MAN´S CELL

- **Genre:** horror short story
- **Reference edition:** Poe, E. A. (1846) The Imp of the Perverse. *The May Flower* magazine.
- **1st edition:** July 1845
- **Themes:** insanity, responsibility, morality, guilt

The Imp of the Perverse was initially written for magazine publication, later being published as a short story, and it is written from the point of view of an unnamed narrator who is awaiting execution for murder. From his cell he explains how and why he has reached this point, outlining the planning and carrying out of the murder and his later confession and expounding his philosophy that all people have within them a perverse imp that compels them to act against their best interests. This short story includes elements of psychology, philosophy, logic and religious mysticism, and can also be read as an apologia by Poe for some of his own irrational behaviour. On initial publication it was poorly received by critics, with complaints that the thinking behind the theory and its explanation were incoherent and that the story structure, half essay, half narrative was confusing for readers.

SUMMARY

This story begins as an essay before becoming a monologue by the narrator addressed to an un-named listener. Like many of the protagonists in Poe's work, it becomes apparent that the narrator in this piece, though he is able to talk lucidly, rationally and even intelligently, is mentally unbalanced and may be completely insane.

TOMORROW I DIE

The setting of the tale is a cell where the unnamed narrator is awaiting his execution the following morning. The story describes the events that have led him to this point. He begins to outline, in a style that is more like a philosophical essay than a short story, his theory about the eponymous imp which has brought him to this point. The language is dense, wordy and often pretentious, with allusions to contemporary ideas on human personality and morality. The narrator suggests that there is actual scientific evidence for the existence of this perverse being within us all: "...as an innate and primitive principle of human action, a paradoxical something, which we may call **perverseness**, for want of a more characteristic term." (p. 13). This impulse, which the narrator characterises as an imp, compels us to act in ways that are self-destructive and explains the seemingly irrational behaviours enacted by all of us at one time or another. This section includes elements of philosophy, phrenology (a system which involved the definition of personality traits by measurement of the skull), transcendentalism, psychology and religion, all of which are propounded by the narrator to support his ideas. He explains that he is a victim of the Imp of the Perverse, which is actually responsible for his present situation.

A PERFECT MURDER

The story then takes on a more familiar narrative style as the actual murder that led the narrator to this cell is described. The dead man was a rich relative and his murder was cunningly planned. The narrator had read about Madame Pilau, a Frenchwoman who almost died after she breathing in smoke from a candle that had been poisoned inadvertently. The narrator's intended victim was known to read in bed every night before he went to sleep, using a candle in a room that was dark and badly ventilated. As such, the narrator describes how he substituted the usual candle for one that he had made himself and added poison to. The victim then inhaled the poison and died. The candle stub was removed by the killer, leaving no trace or evidence of any wrong-doing behind. In effect, he had planned and committed the perfect crime. The murder was deemed by the coroner at the inquest to be an act of God and no blame was attached to the murderer. Subsequently, the narrator gained financially by his actions, inheriting wealth from the victim, and for many years he lived a very comfortable life, sure of his safety. He declares that he enjoyed the fact that he was walking around undetected as much as he enjoyed the money he gained from his crime.

WHEN IN DOUBT...

Years pass, and despite the fact that no one has accused him of committing any crime, the narrator has periods of inner doubt which become increasingly frequent. To counteract these, he begins to use a comforting mantra, saying over and over again "I am safe". This works for a short time and he realises that he is undoubtedly safe unless he openly confesses to the murder: "I am safe – I am safe – yes – if I be not fool enough to make an open confession" (p. 20). These thoughts lead him to consider if he is actually capable of confessing, and this idea becomes increasingly intrusive and obsessive, disrupting his previous security.

THERE IS BLOOD ON MY HANDS

As these thoughts begin to take over his life, the narrator eventually panics and runs into the street, where he draws attention to himself by his bizarre behaviour, and he is finally stopped and questioned by the police. It is at this point that the Imp inside makes itself known and he feels that he must confess, doing so loudly, coherently and publicly. After this he is charged with murder. The confession is the only evidence against him at the trial, but it is more than enough for the jury to find him guilty and for him to be sentenced to execution by hanging.

THE DEVIL MADE ME DO IT

From his cell, the night before he is due to be executed, he blames the Imp of the Perverse for his present situation, claiming that it forced him to confess and to draw attention to his guilt. He is not to blame for his predicament, he tells the reader. And now he will be going to another place.

CHARACTER STUDY

Poe's works often feature very few characters, but *The Imp of the Perverse* is exceptional even by his standards. There really is only one principal character: the unnamed narrator. Others, even the murder victim himself, are barely sketched in and a great deal is left to the reader's imagination.

THE NARRATOR

The narrator of the short story is a convicted murderer, a man of cunning and intelligence, as evinced by the care he has taken in planning and then getting away with the perfect murder. He is greedy and seemingly without a conscience, living for many years on the spoils of his crime, untroubled by any regret for his actions. Indeed, he says that he found the fact that he got away with murder as satisfying as the wealth that the act brought him. He later seems to have been driven slowly mad by subconscious feelings of guilt, a decline that he attributes to the influence of the Imp rather than any pangs of real conscience. He is verbose to the point of annoying the reader: "Had I not been thus prolix, you might either have misunderstood me altogether, or, with the rabble, fancied me mad" (p. 18), and uses this as an example of the perversity of the Imp. He seems to be well read and up to date with the latest philosophical theories about human behaviour, and touches on phrenology and psychology, which he uses to justify his theories. The narrator's apparent decline into insanity means that, although he sees himself as perfectly sane, we cannot fully rely on his version of events.

The narrator never expresses any overt guilt for the murder that he has committed. It is also notable that he appears to view the commission of the murder as entirely logical and understandable – he makes no attempt to blame the murder upon the Imp which he supposes drives him later to publicly confess. We see the story of the murder and subsequent confession only through his eyes, and his only attempt at justification comes when he tries to explain what has driven him to confess: "...I am...one of many uncounted victims of the Imp of the Perverse" (p. 18). The character of the narrator may have represented Poe himself, who led a life that often seemed inexplicably self-destructive, so the narrator can be seen as speaking for the author, justifying some of his rasher actions.

MADAME PILAU

Madame Pilau is a French woman who almost accidentally dies after inhaling smoke from a poisoned candle. It is reading an account of this story that gives the narrator the idea for the murder, and it may even provide the impulse that leads to murder. Although we learn almost nothing about Madame Pilau, her experience underpins the dramatic thrust of the tale.

THE MURDER VICTIM

We are never sure of the real relationship between victim and killer, and we learn little about the murdered person except that they are rich, literate and a creature of habit. The murder is the event on which the theory of the Imp of the Perverse is based.

THE AUDIENCE

We are a silent audience, but one that it is necessary for the narrator to address if the storytelling of the murder is to make sense. We are drawn in by listening to the story as it is told, and by being presented with and then examining the theory he proposes. By accepting or rejecting his justifications for the crimes, the reader builds a relationship with the narrator. The narrator attempts to take us into his confidence and to reduce our feelings of repugnance about the crime and its later concealment by asking us to recall our own experiences of being self-destructive, drawing us together with him as he does so: "We stand upon the brink of a precipice- We peer in to the abyss – we grow sick and dizzy... Unaccountably we remain" (pp. 16-17).

ANALYSIS

A TINY VIGNETTE OF HORROR

The Imp of the Perverse is a difficult story to place categorically in a genre because it has an unusual structure, starting as an essay then reverting to a conventional short story, but most critics broadly agree that it is a tale of horror. The horror genre is generally characterised by elements that repulse or frighten the reader, with a central figure who is often malevolent or evil and with a growing sense of suspense built up through natural or supernatural elements. Poe is an acknowledged master of the genre and uses his skills to great effect in this story.

The main character is a condemned murderer, who has carried out a vile and premeditated murder purely for the sake of getting rich, and has shown a spine-chilling cunning in doing so. The murder is perfect and he has successfully evaded detection for many years. The description of the planning of the murder and its subsequent execution, and the self-serving way that the narrator tries to evade responsibility for his actions, are emphasised by outlining a theory that invites the reader to join him in blaming the Imp of the Perverse for his present predicament: "Examine these and similar actions as we will, we shall find them resulting solely from the spirit of the Perverse" (p. 17). The Imp itself is presented as a supernatural, unsettling being, and as something that is a real entity, playing on the reader's fears of an alien being lurking within them which has the potential of taking over them. According to the narrator, this being is present in us all, waiting to lure us into self-destruction. The suspense is built up as we have to wait to learn exactly why the narrator is in his present predicament, what he has done and why, and to find out his fate, which is revealed in the last sentences in a most brutal way: "Today I wear these chains and am HERE. Tomorrow I shall be fetterless! – BUT WHERE?" (p. 22). The reader is left to imagine the worst.

THIS WAY MADNESS LIES

One of the main themes of the story is the examination of the line between sanity and insanity. Whilst the narrator appears to be rambling and incoherent, especially in the first half of the story, he claims that he is actually completely sane and that his verbosity and erudition are shown in the theory that he outlines. Indeed, his execution of the murder and subsequent behaviour in concealing it seem to reveal a cool intelligence, capable of forward planning and concealment: "It is impossible that any deed could have been wrought with a more thorough deliberation" (p. 18). However, the narrator seems to be driven slowly insane by the repression of what he has done and his behaviour becomes increasingly bizarre. The reader may feel that he ultimately confesses because he has lost his mind, driven mad by feelings of guilt. The narrator begs to differ and blames the confession on the Imp, maintaining that it is this alone that has caused his present situation.

Closely linked to this is the author's examination of the idea of responsibility. If the narrator is indeed responsible for the original murder, his later actions, which clearly show mental instability and cause him to confess, hint that perhaps he was never sane, even at the time of the murder: "I bounded like a madman through the crowded thoroughfares" (p. 21). Indeed, perhaps carrying out a killing of any kind is a sign of insanity. In this case, should he be deemed at all responsible for his actions and treated as a sane person? From the point of view of the narrator, he is not responsible for his confession and so not for his present predicament.

NATURE OR NURTURE?

The theme of nature versus nurture is touched on as well, with Poe referring to scientific theories such as phrenology that deem that personality is innate: "It is a radical, a primitive impulse — elementary" (p. 14). The story seems to suggest that, if the desire to act in a self-destructive way is present in us all, if it is part of human nature, then can any of us be blamed for our impulsive behaviours, any more than we can be blamed for having blue eyes or black hair? In this Poe had a personal interest due to the fact that some of his behaviours, such as alcoholism, seemed irrational and self-destructive. For the modern reader the Imp may also represent signs of illness such as obsessive-compulsive disorder (OCD), and again, can we blame the person who has these conditions for their behaviour? Thus, the story asks us to consider whether, if a person is not responsible for their behaviour, they can be held morally culpable for their actions and the consequences of them.

This tale has a challenging and unexpected structure for the reader. The first part of the story is a densely written essay, drawing on all sorts of sources to outline the theory of the Imp of the Perverse. Some critics at the time complained that it was incoherent, verbose and obscure: "He chases from the wilderness of phrenology into that of transcendentalism then into that of metaphysics generally; then through many weary pages into the open field of inductive philosophy, where he at last corners the poor thing, and then most unmercifully pokes it to death with a long stick" said one reviewer writing in December 1845 in the *Nassau Monthly*. But, this style can also be seen as reflecting the character of the narrator, a man of some intelligence who is yet not entirely sane, drawing on snippets of reading and knowledge and contemporary theories to support his contention of the Imp of the Perverse, and literally swamping readers with ideas in an effort to overwhelm them into agreeing with him. The narrator uses "we" often as he speaks, inviting the reader to become complicit with him, to identify with him and to acknowledge their own experiences of the Imp in their lives: "We could not understand, that is to say, we could not have understood, had the notion of this primum mobile ever obtruded itself; — we could not have understood in what manner it might be made..." (p. 12). Poe cleverly uses capital letters when talking about the Imp, as if it were a real person, a living entity that has corporeal existence. This makes the Imp at once supernatural and natural and creates an unsettling vision for the reader.

The first person narrative perspective draws the reader right into the mind of the murderer, as it does in one of Poe's best-known works, *The Tell-Tale Heart,* and means that we only see the world through his eyes, the eyes of a man who has gone mad. The claustrophobic setting of a cell adds a further layer of horror of the story. Who is he speaking to there? Is it just him and us? The whole gothic setting is powerful and effective.

THE IMP

The Imp itself is a metaphorical device, representing human beings' impulse to self-destruction that the condemned man says is within us all. In contemporary eyes, an imp was seen as a small demon, literally the devil's servant inside of us, and had connotations of evil and malevolence. This would have resonated strongly with readers at the time, most of whom who would believe from their religious upbringing that there was a power for evil in existence that could enter their souls and that drove immoral behaviours.

The story Is rooted very deeply in the social and cultural context of the time. The essay mentions many ideas that were common currency. For example, phrenology, which is the study of human skulls as an indicator of personality, was coming to the fore. Indeed, the whole idea of trying to predict behaviour through science was a burgeoning movement that Poe would have been very aware of. Rationality and religion were beginning to come into conflict in explanations of behaviour. The idea of the subconscious and its role in the repression of unwanted feelings were not common currency and in this Poe was an astute precursor of the ideas of Sigmund Freud (Austrian neurologist and psychoanalyst, 1856-1939). He also mentions metaphysics, which looks at the origins of all matter, and the Kabala, a Jewish teaching that looks at hidden meanings in Hebrew scripture.

Poe himself showed signs of the influence of the Imp of the Perverse throughout his life in his relationships both personal and professional, in his disastrous managing of his financial affairs and in his own addictions, and the story can also be seen as an exercise in self-explanation, or in reneging on taking any responsibility for his actions and their consequences. Equally, the story can be read as a deliberate attempt to provoke those who had annoyed him, challenging those publishers and editors with whom he was often in conflict.

Further exploration of this impulse was evident in the revelations of the narrators in other Poe short stories including *The Black Cat.* The phrase that is the title of the story has entered into popular culture and even the subject of psychological papers, and is sometimes referred to in discussions about OCD, anxiety, poor impulse control and intrusive thoughts.

FURTHER REFLECTION

SOME QUESTIONS TO THINK ABOUT...

- How far do you agree with Poe when he refers to the subconscious as something that controls our actions and behaviours?
- The first part of the story is written in the style of an essay. The second part is written as a more conventional narrative. Do they work together as a short story? Why/why not?
- "With certain minds, under certain conditions, it becomes absolutely irresistible" (p. 14). Is it ever entirely true that we have no control over our actions?
- Does the story persuade you that the Imp of the Perverse serves any useful function for humans?
- How far do the events in Poe's own life reflect the influence of the Imp of the Perverse?
- Are our actions influenced more by nature or by nurture?

- How does Poe use language to communicate to the reader the idea that narrator is insane?
- Does the absence of any other voices in the story add to or subtract from the narrative? Explain your answer.

We want to hear from you!
Leave a comment on your online library
and share your favourite books on social media!

FURTHER READING

REFERENCE EDITION

- Poe, E. A. (1846) The Imp of the Perverse. *The May Flower* magazine.

- This work is now in the public domain and the full text of this version of the story is available on the website of the Edgar Allen Poe Society of Baltimore at https://www.eapoe.org/works/tales/impb.htm

REFERENCE STUDIES

- The Edgar Allen Poe Society of Baltimore maintains a website (https://www.eapoe.org/index.htm) which provides detailed biographical information about the writer, critical analysis of his writing and the text of those of his works which are now in the public domain.

ADDITIONAL SOURCES

- Montague, C. (2015) *Edgar Allan Poe: The Strange Man Standing Deep in the Shadows*. New York: Chartwell Books.

- Quinn, A. H. (1941) *Edgar Allan Poe: A Critical Biography*. New York: D. Appleton-Century Company Incorporated.

ADAPTATIONS

- In 1975 the British Broadcasting Corporation (BBC) broadcast a television adaptation of this work. This was titled *The Imp of the Perverse* and was written by Andrew Davies, starred Gerald Cross and formed part of the Centre Play series of original plays.

- Several graphic novels have been based on this work, including the Graphic Classics series which has featured a number of adaptations of Poe short stories.

- In 2018 a kick-starter project featuring a role-playing game (RPG) titled *Imp of the Perverse* was announced. The game was created by Nathan D. Paoletta and promises to provide "a psychological horror game of monster hunting in Jacksonian Gothic America."

MORE FROM BRIGHTSUMMARIES.COM

- Reading guide – *The Black Cat* by Edgar Allan Poe.

- Reading guide – *The Fall of the House of Usher* by Edgar Allan Poe.

- Reading guide – *The Gold-Bug* by Edgar Allan Poe.
- Reading guide – *The Masque of the Red Death* by Edgar Allan Poe.
- Reading guide – *The Murders in the Rue Morgue* by Edgar Allan Poe.
- Reading guide – *The Purloined Letter* by Edgar Allan Poe.
- Reading guide – *The Tell-Tale Heart* by Edgar Allan Poe.

www.brightsummaries.com

Ebook EAN: 9782808017701

Paperback EAN: 9782808017718

Legal Deposit: D/2019/12603/52

Cover: © Primento

Digital conception by Primento, the digital partner of
publishers.